Working with The Venture Scout Training Scheme

A Handbook for Venture Scout Leaders and Unit Executive Committees

Edited by
Hazel Chewter

Contributors
Ian Astle, Jock Barr,
Andrew Bollington, Julia Bowles,
David Bull, Roger Haywood,
Philip Heath, Nick Higgins,
Marilyn Hudson, Steve Peck,
Sue Peck, Gareth Roberts,
James Sime, Mick Stocks,
Hamish Stout, Graham Wilson

*Designed by students in the
Department of Typography &
Graphic Communication,
University of Reading*

First Edition 1987
First Printing July 1987

Printed by the Pindar Group of Companies

Although we appreciate that many
Venture Scout Units have female
Members, for ease of reading we
have referred to Venture Scouts
as 'he' throughout this series of
booklets.

Contents

Introduction

Working with the Venture Scout Training Scheme is aimed at the Venture Scout Leader and the Unit Executive Committee. It is intended that, within these pages, an explanation and understanding of the Training Scheme will emerge. You will find an explanation of the thoughts behind each section as well as programme application ideas and suggestions on the all important *how to make it work*.

This guide does not repeat all the examples given in the main volume *The Venture Scout Training Scheme* nor is it intended to be a book for Venture Scouts to use as an ideas library. It is hoped that this publication will be used in conjunction with the main volume to encourage Venture Scouts to participate in the Venture Scout Award and the Queen's Scout Award and to assist Units in the preparation of worthwhile Unit programmes.

A Training Scheme of one sort or another has always been an integral part of Scouting. Such Schemes have been designed to broaden the young person's experience through a multitude of experiences and interests.

The Training Scheme for Venture Scouts is flexible. The Venture Scout Award and the Queen's Scout Award can be tailored to meet the needs of all Members and almost any activity or interest can be incorporated. There are no absolute standards, these are decided by the Unit Executive Com-

mittee and in many instances adapted to the potential of the individuals concerned.

In planning the Unit programme, the Unit Executive Committee should ensure that there is ample opportunity for every Venture Scout to progress within the Training Scheme. The Unit Executive Committee should also ensure that the programme contains items which are attractive to all the Members – the youngest through to the eldest, male and female, able-bodied and handicapped. But, it may, from time to time, decide to include some which appeal to a minority only.

The Venture Scout Award and the Queen's Scout Award are concerned with individual physical, mental and spiritual development. The Members of the Unit will see the same programme in a variety of ways, using it as appropriate to qualify for the different sections of the Awards – as decided by each Member – in conjunction with the Unit Executive Committee.

In order to monitor the progress of individuals the Unit Executive Committee will want to record the achievements of each Member of the Unit. How this is done is very much a matter for the Unit Executive Committee. Each Member of the Unit will, of course, have – and will update – his own *Venture Scout Record Book* which could be presented at investiture.

There are two principles which an Executive Committee should take into account – genuine sustained effort is required with growing interest in the subject *and* some positive indication of progress, application or achievement. This is harder to assess than an absolute standard but it is much fairer. Some young people would be able to achieve a set standard with no effort whilst others might struggle for months. In every case, the standard expected will depend upon whether the Venture Scout is commencing the activity as a beginner or whether some experience has already been gained.

A reasonable standard for a complete beginner would not be sufficient for a person with some previous experience. This second principle may be likened to climbing a ladder – for an activity new to the Venture Scout the appropriate starting point would be at the bottom of the ladder and personal progress for the Venture Scout Award might be climbing three rungs in order to achieve a reasonable standard. For someone who has prior experience of the chosen activity, a starting point might be the middle of the ladder –

again climbing three rungs in order to achieve satisfactory personal progress.

When established guidelines or standards do not exist, it is clear that certain sections of the Venture Scout Award and the Queen's Scout Award cannot be assessed in terms of hard and fast goals. Alternative avenues of approach must be explored, each Venture Scout's achievement must be judged in isolation and, ultimately, it will be the Members of the Unit Executive Committee who will decide on the level of achievement. Each Unit has to make its own decisions but the Programme and Training Department at Gilwell Park is happy to help.

The contents of this publication are, mainly, a compilation of the work and thoughts of a number of Leaders from all over the country and our grateful thanks are given to them.

Please use this 'guide' in any way you see fit to assist and encourage Venture Scouts to participate in the Training Scheme with enthusiasm, boldness and success.

Some background

The ethos behind the Venture Scout Training Scheme is to use progressive training as a vehicle towards the physical, mental and spiritual development of young people so that they may take a constructive place in society, taking account of the needs and abilities of each individual.

The Training Scheme is designed to be wide in choice so that each Venture Scout can choose items that are of interest within each Section. Once the Members have chosen the items that they wish to do they should work out how best to achieve the highest possible standard within that area. Thus different achievement levels will be reached for each Venture Scout.

The Training Scheme is designed to be self-assessed by each individual Venture Scout and each Member is responsible for setting his own goals. Members should be encouraged to aim high so that they achieve as much as they can, and feel that they are being stretched.

There is a great deal of Unit Executive Committee participation. They are the arbitrators of the Scheme and they are the awarding body. Their role is to evaluate individual progress and development, basing their decisions on the knowledge of the individuals concerned – the ability and potential of each Venture Scout. The Unit Executive Committee may decide to appoint someone to assess a particular section of the Award Scheme.

Within the Scheme is a vast number of programme ideas so that Venture Scouts should be able to complete the Membership Badge and Venture Scout Award by playing an active part in Unit Meetings and events. The natural lead-on from this is to tackle the Queen's Scout Award, becoming increasingly responsible and actively involved in the workings of the Unit, other Sections of the Movement and outside agencies.

It is not necessary for a Member to be a 'super-Venture Scout' to achieve the Badge and Awards. All that is required is that the Member plays a *full part* in the life of an active Venture Scout Unit. By good programme planning the individual can, with the active assistance of the Unit Executive Committee, Venture Scout Leader and Assistant Venture Scout Leaders, gain the Membership Badge and both Awards. The Venture Scout will not do this if he is just a passive 'social'

Member as the requirements often ask for an active involvement in the affairs of the Unit and the outside world.

It is quite possible for individual Venture Scouts to gain the Venture Scout Award within 18 months to two years of joining the Section and quite reasonable to expect the same Member to gain the Queen's Scout Award within 12–18 months of that, thus a Venture Scout joining at 15½ years could, with active involvement, expect to gain the Queen's Scout Award by the 19th birthday.

Having said all this it should, however, be stated that there will always be some Venture Scouts who will join for comradeship, some social activity, a break from pressure of home or school and so on. We must not expect each and every Venture Scout to want to be a Queen's Scout, or even a Venture Scout Award holder. Some will just want to belong.

The theme that lies behind the whole Section is that learning can be enjoyable. Venture Scouts should be able to gain skills of many types whilst they enjoy themselves. We are not a school for 15 to 20 year olds, we are part of a voluntary youth service and as such should create opportunities for learning rather than learning with extra-curricular activities.

Most Venture Scouts join because they want to be with a friend, friends or a group of young people with whom they identify. They don't join to be a Venture Scout specifically. Thus, the learning they will experience through the progressive Training Scheme has to be found within an enjoyable, active programme. Through the programme they will, if they wish, and if they are encouraged, find opportunity to sample the outdoors, service to others, comradeship, fun, adventure and all the other facets that the Venture Scout Training Scheme offers.

Leading the Unit

The Unit Executive Committee and the Venture Scout Leader have a specific role to play within the Training Scheme. Some suggestions for self-preparation are indicated below.

1 *Get to know yourself*
What kind of person are you? It is important to know yourself and to know what others think of you. As Leaders you will be trusted with a position of authority. How this authority is used and how responsibilities are discharged is important to the Unit and to other observers.

2 *Get to know other Members*
As Leaders you have to work with others, it is not a good idea to do everything yourself. In the first place that would take too much time and, secondly, having Members to help is a good way of encouraging and training them.

3 *Get to know the job*
Get to know what is expected of the Unit Executive Committee. Make use of all the resources available. The Venture Scout Leader, other Leaders, Unit Executive Committee Members, Unit Members, parents and other contacts can all be of assistance.

4 *Always have a plan*
Know clearly what the Unit wishes to achieve so that at all stages you understand the situation and are able to provide some direction. This does not mean that the Unit Executive Committee have to make all of the decisions – Members should be encouraged to make suggestions and to give ideas. If Members are not forthcoming with ideas the Unit Executive Committee will have to provide sound suggestions having thought them out in advance. This will give the Unit Members confidence in the Leadership.

Techniques for effective leadership

1 *Share the work*
Use Members for certain tasks. Be able to recognise those who are more skilful than others. Delegate leadership roles. This will free the Unit Executive Committee to do other things and indicate to the Members that you have confidence in them. Find out who is good at what and who can lead this or that.

2 *Don't leave things to chance*
Things often happen because people
work hard to make them happen.
If plans do not get off the ground it
may be because you, as a Leader, have
not ensured that everybody was playing their part. When Members take on
tasks, leave them to carry them out but
make periodic checks to ensure that
all is going well. Support and encourage them.

3 *Be a good listener*
Pay close attention to what is said by
Members, learn to ask useful questions
and try to be aware of what is left
unsaid. In this way you may be able
to judge how you are seen by the
Members.

4 *Be on time*
Be first at a Meeting or activity, have
the work done ahead of time, start
Meetings on time and your example
will be picked up by the Members.

5 *Make the best use of time*
Everyone has many things to do.
Whilst some may choose to waste
their own time it is inefficient and
thoughtless to waste other people's
time.

6 *Be honest*
Leaders must be honest. They may be
called upon to make decisions, judge-
ments or express opinions which
appear to go against a friend or other
individual. If such action is required,
be firm and decisive. Explain the
reasons behind the decisions.

7 *Keep a sense of humour*
Stay cheerful, keep calm and always
look for the best side. Remember,
Venture Scouting is meant to be **fun**.

Venture Scouting and the handicapped

Venture Scouting is about many things – enjoyment, fellowship, responsibility, challenge and rewards are amongst the most obvious. People with handicaps wish to experience these things just like everybody else. Many Units have proved for themselves that the problems presented by Members who have physical or even mental disabilities can be overcome given the will. Of course extra planning and sometimes extra efforts are required but the gains of getting to know a person with a handicap really well far outweigh the disadvantages.

Venture Scouts with a handicap should be encouraged and enabled to undertake the Training Scheme in its entirety as outlined in this handbook. Often, things will be tougher for them, they may need more time, more help, more resources but whenever it is at all possible, the Unit Executive Committee should encourage them to 'have a go'.

Safety

Commonsense will tell you where to be cautious. Obviously people must never be put into dangerous situations and the maxim 'better safe than sorry' must always apply. It is important to think about the risks in respect of someone who is not fully able-bodied or mentally intact. Discuss the matter with him, maybe with his parents,

if you are not sure. Your Assistant District Commissioner (Handicapped) or Assistant County/Area Commissioner (Handicapped) will also be able to give some guidance.

Standards

Hardly any of us can do everything as well as we would like. Scouting requires very few absolute standards of performance. What the Association does want is that people 'do their best'. If a person's handicap means that they can only perform half as well as the rest of us, that's ok, if he has had a go, joined in and done as well as he can. The Unit Executive Committee should accept that the necessary standard has been obtained. **But** handicapped people are not looking for a soft ride. Some of the activities in this book are challenging and tough and it should be so for everyone, within the limits of their capabilities.

Alternatives

Sometimes safety dictates or the handicap will simply prevent an individual from trying a particular activity. Fair enough, there are lots of alternatives. The Unit Executive Committee has the power to vary the requirements, bearing in mind that something of an equal degree of demand should be substituted. Again consultation with the person concerned, perhaps the parents, certainly

the Assistant District Commissioner (Handicapped), is advisable.

Any questions?

The Assistant District Commissioner (Handicapped) or Assistant County/ Area Commissioner (Handicapped) is there to help you, don't be afraid to ask his or her advice. If you are stuck, drop a line to the Headquarters Commissioner for the Handicapped at Gilwell Park.

Programme planning

If the Unit Executive Committee looks at the suggestions given under all three parts of the Venture Scout Training Scheme, they will, with thought and local adaptation, be able to plan programmes for the Unit for years and years!

The three sections cover all aspects of physical, mental and spiritual development as well as social inter-action and inter-personal relationships. The Membership Badge and the two Awards encourage active and passive 'in Headquarters' programmes, visiting speakers, visits, short and long weekends, full expeditions, specialist activities, cultural and creative pursuits and so on. Because every Unit is different, due to the Membership, locality, finance and

other factors, the programme will be different and thus if we have about 4,300 Units we can expect to find about 4,300 different weekly programmes – and all at the same time!

The Unit Executive Committee should, first of all, consider the needs of the individual when planning the programme of the Unit. Unit Members must be asked for their ideas, canvassed about ideas generated by the Executive Committee and asked to consider how ideas for their Venture Scout Award or Queen's Scout Award choice can be added into the weekly programme.

Most Members will have skills which can be utilised in the weekly programme – some may be reluctant to show off their abilities but others may be quite willing to help.

Underlying the plans of the Venture Scout Leader and the Unit Executive Committee should always be the thought that if the needs and requirements of the Members are not sought out and met then the management may well lose the interest of those same Members.

The Unit Executive Committee will no doubt wish to find other programme ideas. The Venture Scout Section has a number of publications to assist in the search for a balanced programme. SCOUTING Magazine offers, monthly, a host of suggestions and, of course, other Units, the Assistant District Commissioner (Venture

Scouts) and other Scouters and Unit Executive Committees can be of help.

In addition to the contents of the publications for the Venture Scout Section, Units will, of course, have their own particular favourites, contacts and facilities. These factors will add to the Unit's weekly Meetings.

The Unit Executive Committee or a Unit-in-council could spend a very useful afternoon once a year finalising the themes for the coming year, the main contents to go under each theme, the experts they will need to recruit and the equipment they will need to obtain, borrow and so on, leaving the detailed planning to the Member(s) responsible.

If the main points of the programme are decided upon the 'meat can be added to the bone' by the Members using the Venture Scout publications to find suitable ideas to fill the evenings or weekends. If items are to be found under the Award headings then so much the better for the Members organising as they could use them for their own personal progress.

The programme for a Venture Scout Unit should contain elements of fun, adventure, physical effort, brain use, spirituality, stupidity and enjoyment. If the mix is correct, the balance of ideas will assist in retaining Venture Scout Members but, if it is not, the Unit will find the Membership falling away. A Unit is only as good as its programme.

The occasional evening led by a Leader is not a bad idea especially if the programme content is novel and possibly a secret. However, the programme must be well thought out, well planned and well executed so that it can be used as an example for the Unit Executive Committee and Members. The Leader should not, however, run, or be expected to run, a lot of programmes unless the Unit has just been formed and the transition of power is occurring gradually. In short:

▷ What are the needs of the Members?

▷ Plan about 12 months in advance (general plans)

▷ Residential activities and 'major' events should go into the programme first

▷ Choose themes

▷ Select theme items

▷ Plan three months in detail

▷ Use handbooks, magazines and journals for ideas

▷ Encourage Members to work for the Awards through the programmes

▷ Ensure a variety of programme ideas

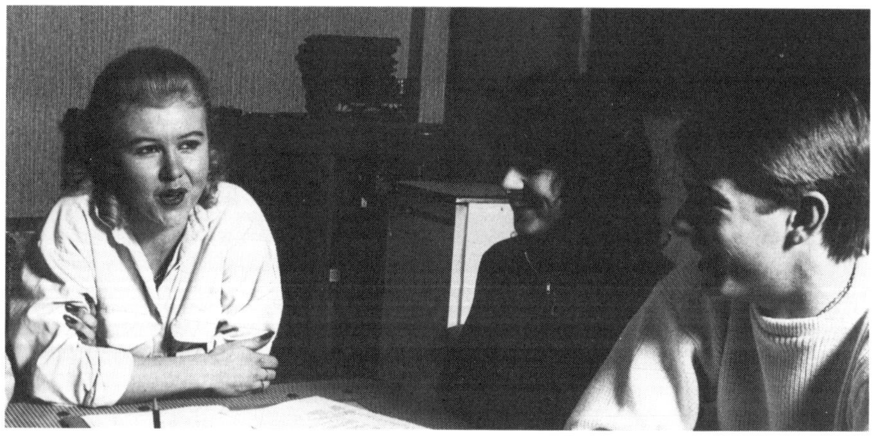

- ▷ Encourage Members to run weekly programmes
- ▷ Encourage Members to run camps, events and expeditions
- ▷ Use programmes run by Leaders occasionally
- ▷ Insert the occasional surprise
- ▷ Avoid repeating the same programme
- ▷ Plan ahead
- ▷ Evaluate afterwards

  and

- ▷ Always invite guests well in advance
- ▷ Expect some programmes to fail
- ▷ Don't always be in the Head-quarters (get outside!)
- ▷ Hold the occasional 'silly' event
- ▷ Contact the Scout Troop for joint programmes
- ▷ Invite potential new Members to attend
- ▷ Include training activities
- ▷ Include service activities
- ▷ Try new pursuits (see what happens!)
- ▷ Meet with other Units
- ▷ Get involved with the community
- ▷ *Let people know what your Unit is doing.*

The Venture Scout Membership Badge

Rule 121 ii
The Venture Scout Membership Badge

To be passed under arrangements made by the Unit Executive Committee.

This badge takes the form of the World Membership Badge, i.e. the Arrowhead Badge on a purple background surrounded by a rope in a circle, tied in a reef knot at the bottom.

Requirements

Action
Take part in a sufficient number of activities with the Unit to ensure that you are aware of the responsibilities and implications of Membership.

Note:
Scouts who have worked on the Explorer or Chief Scout's Awards and who have been associated with Venture Scouts in obtaining parts of these Awards qualify for this section as determined by the Unit Executive Committee.

Understanding
Show that you understand and support the aims and international aspects of the Scout Movement and that you know how your Unit is managed and what is expected of you as a Venture Scout.

Commitment
Know, understand and accept the Scout Promise and Law.

Note:
A Scout may qualify for this badge during the three months prior to his transfer from the Scout Troop.

The requirements laid out above will offer Venture Scout Leaders and Unit Executive Committees an opening for 'links' between the Scout Troop(s) and Unit. The *note* concerning the older Scout should encourage Units to plan events and activities which will help the transfer from Troop to Unit.

A large measure of freedom is provided under the requirements so that this introductory badge can be aimed at the needs of each potential Venture Scout, whether they be from a Scout Troop or from outside.

Here is the opportunity for the Chairman of the Unit Executive Committee and the Venture Scout Leader to get to know the potential Members by getting them to join in Unit activities and by having a conversation with the prospective recruit – but remember, conversations are a two-way exercise!

The invitation to a weekend activity, involvement in Unit Meetings (preferably a well planned version) or a fund raising exercise or similar, will all add to the potential recruits' understanding of the Unit and its Members.

If a new recruit is expected to visit the Unit it is not good enough to expect him to turn up and be immediately integrated with the Members. The potential Member will have to be met, looked after and made to feel welcome. Units can often be rather strange and daunting to the newcomer.

If we expect the potential recruit to understand and support the Aim and the international aspect of the Movement, somebody, preferably a Unit Member, must explain to them what we mean. The same must be said for a knowledge of how the Unit is managed and what is expected of the individual within the Unit. It must not be expected that knowledge is gained by simply walking through the door!

We also ask the new Members to know, understand and accept the Scout Promise and Law. We cannot expect any young person to enter into this commitment unless they are made fully aware of what they are agreeing to! Careful explanation needs to be given by an experienced Member who is very sure of his own commitment.

It is not necessary for the Unit to set up a formal interview to see if the recruits are suitable for Membership and to test their knowledge – such arrangements are much more likely to put new Members off. A quiet chat to see how much understanding the potential Venture Scouts have of Membership implications, international aspects, Unit management along with a knowledge and acceptance of the Scout Promise and Law, should be all that is required.

Venture Scouts will have different levels of understanding and acceptance and this must be borne in mind when talking to new Members before they are given the Membership Badge. Each young person is different and so differences in the approach and personal beliefs must be accepted.

A simple investiture ceremony without any embarrassing features should follow this initial stage during which the Membership of the Unit is conferred and the badge presented.

Note:
'Camp Christening' of any kind is a pastime for bullies and has no place in the Scout Movement.

The Venture Scout Award

Rule 123
The Venture Scout Award
To be passed under arrangements made by the Unit Executive Committee.
A white 'V' with a laurel wreath and an Arrowhead badge on a brown background.

Requirements

This Award is intended to provide a balanced programme for each Venture Scout and for the Unit as a whole. The Venture Scout should then use the experience to undertake responsibility within the Unit. Full details of possible activities and standards of assessment are to be found in *The Venture Scout Training Scheme* published by The Scout Association. To achieve the Venture Scout Award, a Venture Scout must have made personal progress and widened his experience and skill in each of the following areas of personal growth.

Activity
Acquiring new skills, developing self-confidence, improving physical fitness and well being through active involvement in indoor and outdoor pursuits.

Community Involvement
Making contact with people within the community having real needs, and working towards meeting those needs, to the benefit of the community.

Creativity
Self-expression through creative, artistic or design activities.

Independence
Acquiring practical life skills, developing socially, reaching a measure of independence towards the future.

International Awareness
Learning about other peoples, their cultures and values and becoming a more caring member of our multicultural society.

Leadership
Participating in training for leadership and undertaking some measure of responsibility within the Unit.

Outdoors and Environment
Combining outdoor activities of any nature with practical effort in caring for the environment.

Relationships
Facing up to the challenge of learning to live with other people in mutual harmony.

Values
Forming personal attitudes and opinions on issues and learning to respect and tolerate the views of others

Notes:

(i) A particular activity may only count for one section of the Award.

(ii) Recent achievements gained through the Scout Section may, at the discretion of the Unit Executive Committee, count towards parts of this Award.

(iii) Older Scouts, whilst in the Scout Troop, are encouraged to join with Members of the Unit in undertaking parts of this Award and can count this experience when they eventually join the Unit. However, it is intended that most of the Award requirements shall be completed within, and as a Member of, the Venture Scout Unit.

(iv) Venture Scouts may undertake any number of sections of the Award at the same time

How to make the Venture Scout Award work

There are many, many types of Venture Scout Unit and, thus, Unit programmes, but the Venture Scouts themselves can often be put into two general categories when discussing the Training Scheme:

(a) the Award group
(b) the 'I'm not interested in Awards' group.

Whilst it is recognised that there will always be a small proportion of the latter group, the numbers can be greatly reduced by well planned programmes which are based upon the natural interests of the Members and formed from the ideas within the publication *The Venture Scout Training Scheme*.

If a Unit Executive Committee plans a set of programmes (on a term or seasonal basis or as a build-up to an event or activity) they can use the headings within the Venture Scout Award for guidance. Members can be given roles within the programme, they can assist the planning, they can be involved with the results of the planning and they can be instrumental in making it work.

A programme needs a beginning, a middle and an end. The beginning is concerned with the plan, the resources (human and material), the timescale, Members taking part and so on. The middle is the programme itself – how it is run, getting people involved and making sure it goes as it is supposed to. The end concerns the evaluation of the programme – how it went, what went wrong, what was right and any alterations for future use. If the Unit Executive Committee plans specific involvement for certain Members then those Members can achieve part of the Award within the context of the programme.

On the next page are two suggested themes which could be used as programme ideas. Themes can be specific or general. They can last a number of weeks or a number of months. They can involve a few people doing a lot of things or a lot of people doing one or two things each.

Theme
Build up to summer camp

Weekly programme items:

Activity
Hike/physical pursuit/Charge Certificate/
Youth Hostel

Community Involvement
First aid/rescue training

Creativity
Cookery/ciné/video/photography/act of
worship

Independence
Economic cooking/general cooking/
managing money/insurance

International Awareness
Languages/culture/food/local contact

Leadership
Run the camp/take a specific role

Outdoors and Environment
Environmental expedition/conservation
project/map changes

Relationships
Organising with others/camp committee/
camp newsletter/programme service

Values
Act of Worship/different faiths/cultures

Theme
The practicalities of life

Weekly programme items:

Activity
Fitness training/gardening

Community Involvement
First aid/careers and jobs/rescue skills

Creativity
Design/painting/craftwork

Independence
Managing money/plumbing/budgeting/
youth employment

International Awareness
Pen pals/Mah-Jong and so on/
languages

Leadership
Run a series of evenings on one or more of
the above.

Outdoors and Environment
Cultivation/recycling/waste treatment

Relationships
Dinner party/committee work/
communications

Values
Court visits/standards/moral issue film
or play

The Member or Members who organise or run the evenings are the ones who complete that area of the Venture Scout Award and it should be obvious to other non-organising Members that this is the case. The Unit Executive Committee should be satisfied before, during and after the programme that the criteria for good planning and development are being met. These criteria may be:

▷ Starting point

▷ Targets

▷ Was the programme well planned?

▷ Was the programme well thought out?

▷ Who did the work?

▷ Were others involved?

▷ Was it successful, or if not, why not?

▷ Did the Member(s) concerned learn from the experience?

▷ Was it challenging enough?

▷ Did the Member 'stretch' himself?

▷ Were the assessing standards applied?

If all the criteria applied show that the Member 'did the necessary' when taking into account his abilities then the Unit Executive Committee should award that area of the Venture Scout Award to the Member(s) concerned. If the Unit Executive Committee has doubts then they should find out what went wrong and suggest modification and alterations with the Member(s)

concerned. Here it may well be necessary for the Venture Scout Leader to become involved as the Member(s) may well be a friend of the Unit Executive Committee and a difficult situation could be avoided. (They may have taken the advice of an appointed 'expert').

Thus, the application of mind, initiative and imagination can enable individual Venture Scouts to progress through the Venture Scout Award by adopting the basic ideas in *The Venture Scout Training Scheme*. The support, guidance and active assistance of the Unit Executive Committee and Venture Scout Leader will thus enable more Venture Scouts to climb the rungs of the ladder which leads to the Venture Scout Award.

Activity

Venture Scouts are expected to participate in some physical activities – after all the word 'physical' is highlighted in the Aim of The Scout Association.

Activities are important in very many areas of personal development – improving physical fitness and stamina, heightening alertness and co-ordination, creating team spirit and awareness, building self-confidence and so on. To get the most out of an activity programme there is the need to think carefully about achievement levels but in setting these the capabilities and potential of the individual are all important. It is unreasonable to expect every individual to attain the same fixed goal. So, for example, a programme objective should not be for all three members of a group to swim three miles each, but for members of the group to attain a collective total of nine miles, with each individual attempting to put in a personal best to contribute to that overall total.

Having considered programme balance, thought must be given to placing the activities into a useful context. This means not having a series of one-off activities but rather linking a series of activities to achieve a particular purpose such as a series of activities making up a training programme towards an expedition or towards a sponsored non-stop badminton game.

Expeditions and personal survival

This goal could be a three-day expedition to the nearest National Park or a more ambitious expedition overseas. It could be with four or more Members of the Unit or with the majority of the Unit. Whatever the Membership, duration or location, the preparation is a valuable and essential part of that expedition and in itself a worthwhile programme.

Moors, Hills and Mountains

There is a set of requirements which have to be met. A visit from your local Mountaineering Adviser would be a good starting point for this kind of programme.

As well as learning particular skills, Members will come to depend on each other as soon as they enter the remote part of the location. As well as the value of the achievement felt in this kind of activity, there is a real bond which grows within the group – especially if the going gets tough, due to weather conditions. Having said that, under no circumstances should the situation be forced into being tough in the hope of bringing about that development. Under those circumstances many individuals can be destroyed in terms of self-confidence and their attitude to Venture Scouting and the hills will never be the same again. This particular point, of course, applies to other activities

which have personal and risk
thresholds pushed too far too quickly.

Rock climbing

This activity requires quite different
skills to those for general mountaineering and they are skills which
make real physical and mental
demands. In particular, rock climbing
requires Members to work with, and
place trust in, each other and that, in
the same way, makes them realise that
others are also depending on them.

Caving

Like rock climbing, caving is a skilled
activity and Form CAVE must be held
by the group leader. A great deal of
initial training must be carried out
before entering the cave. For example,
a caving ladder can be suspended
from a tree to provide training in the
many special techniques that this
sport involves.

Sport

The word 'sport' often implies keen
competition, but this does not have to
be so. Sport is a physical recreation
which is to be enjoyed. Having said
that, sport does offer the opportunity
of providing yardsticks as a means of
measuring a Unit Member's performance.

Water activities

A wide range of activities can be linked
with this particular theme and nation-
ally recognised qualifications (British
Canoe Union, Royal Yachting Association, Amateur Swimming Association
and so on) can be gained whilst enjoy-
ing the benefits of these activities.

As part of a programme of water
activities there is a need to consider
Members' safety and well-being so the
policy of The Scout Association with
regard to water based activities should
be understood and followed particularly in respect of charge and boat

certificates. This might be achieved by inviting a local Water Activities Adviser to a Unit Meeting and exploring the resources and knowledge which are available locally.

Air activities

It is true that air activities can be limited because of availability and cost. However, it is possible to include air activities in a programme if there is an interest and determination. If ever an opportunity presents itself it should be seriously considered as a possibility for the programme.

The nature of these activities is such that expert tuition and guidance must be sought. The efforts made in setting up air activities in the programme will be rewarded by an exhilarating experience for Unit Members.

New skills

There will be times when the Unit programmes fall into a rut which seems difficult to get out of. Perhaps one solution is to have a brainstorming session and create a long list of activities – everything goes on this list (well, almost everything!).

Ask each Member to place a tick alongside all the activities that he has never attempted before. From this list of activities make up a three month programme introducing individuals, or groups, to new skills.

The introduction to this section emphasised that assessment of physical activities should be on personal development and improvement rather than on fixed goals. Having said that, it is easy to fall into the trap of thinking in terms of fitness and skill levels, due to the nature of this section.

Personal development, or progress, call it what you will, in activities is very much about development in maturity, attitude of mind, reliability, self-confidence and a whole host of other characteristics.

Appreciation of and respect for others and their skills along with self-discipline and personal training all play a part in the mental and spiritual development of young people. The problem is that the activity section of the Venture Scout Award is often looked at in a 'tough guy' way and the developmental characteristics in other areas are ignored.

Community Involvement

From the time we came into this world we have been a member of the 'community'. This could then have developed with pre-school education and continued with contact with school friends, teachers and neighbours. By the time Venture Scouts are 16 they may have widened their experience to include clubs and societies, they may also have taken part in community projects through school or may have a personal interest in some aspect of community life. Venture Scouting is part of the same community and therefore the community is a very important part of our programme. We cannot operate in isolation and adequate training is essential to make our work worthwhile. This means Venture Scout Units and individual Venture Scouts must create as many opportunities as possible to become directly involved in service to the community.

Venture Scouts accept as part of their Promise that they will do their best to 'help other people'. Community involvement is a way of putting that Promise into action. It also provides an opportunity for the Venture Scouts to have direct contact with people outside their immediate environment to improve their understanding and broaden their experience of commun-

ity life. Much of this contact will involve putting other people first, learning to overcome prejudices and giving real, sustained commitment to others. On the face of it, helping other people is a practical activity. The true benefit (mentally and spiritually) comes from working with other people.

Activity in itself will be of little benefit unless we can see what has been achieved. We would hope that involvement in the community would increase a Venture Scout's awareness of:

▷ The need to work *with* people

▷ Recognising and understanding special needs

▷ Identifying their own strengths and weaknesses

▷ The needs of other people through service involvement

▷ Society outside his immediate social circle

▷ The need for caring and sharing in the community

▷ The need for a balanced view and attitude which might be contrary to the norm.

When assessing a Venture Scout under this section the thoughts that should come to the mind of the Unit Executive Committee and Venture Scout Leader are: 'Did the Venture Scout identify a need within the community and was some kind of target

formulated so that the result could be measured within a given timescale?' Did the Venture Scout concerned work out a plan? Did the Venture Scout work out the necessary financial, material and human resources that would be needed to complete the job? How effective was the plan and could it have been improved? Did the individual Members make a sufficient effort? Was the project interesting and of a suitable quality? What personal development occurred for the Venture Scout concerned?'

Creativity

What does the term 'creative' conjure up in a Venture Scout's mind? It can cover many areas but they would all have a common theme running through them which could perhaps be summed up in the word 'imagination'. You will also find that the word 'creative' is linked with words such as innovative, inventive, original and inspirational.

This Section is included in the Venture Scout Award because the personal characteristics described in the words relating to 'creativity' are the ones that each and every Venture Scout will need to be able to demonstrate in order to really develop their lives and personalities. This will apply whoever they are and whatever their lot in life. Some of them have, or will develop, an artistic flair, others will take some form of responsibility for organisations or people and will need to react to that responsibility in a creative, imaginative way as well as in a caring, sensitive style while others will have much leisure time on their hands (perhaps due to illness or unemployment).

The possible activities in this section of the Award are many and varied. They will cover a wide range of subjects. The music listened to, the books read, the films and plays seen, the clothes which are worn. All of these are the result of creative thought on the part of someone.

Creative activities are designed to help and encourage the development of mental and dexterous skills and develop imaginative artistic and creative abilities. This will enable each Venture Scout to fulfil his responsibilities to others and make imaginative use of his time.

Often a Venture Scout will find a need for inner discipline in the activity chosen. The Member will need to concentrate on detail and will often have to listen to other people's views. Imagine the production of a play or musical without self-discipline, detailed concentration and the views of others being heard. In creative activities, especially stage productions, a special moment often occurs – it may be in the applause or during a pause in the action. These moments are to be savoured and remembered.

In this section of the Venture Scout Award, programme ideas are presented as activities that can be undertaken by a Member working with, or at least presenting to, small groups of Venture Scouts. This is because it is not only important to develop imaginative and creative talents but it is part of creativity to be able to communicate those skills in an interesting and stimulating way to other people, including Unit Members.

The list of ideas in *The Venture Scout Training Scheme* is not exhaustive by any means, but gives examples of the

wide range of activities which can be used by individuals or groups as part of their creative development or with a little adaptation, by the whole Unit during one of its programme evenings or other event.

The programme ideas in *The Venture Scout Training Scheme* can be used to provide a base line for developing a standard for an activity – but you will need to modify each one by specifying the measure of the standard to be reached by Members undertaking the activity.

In the end, the Unit or Executive Committee must remember that the standard to be attained must be personal to the Members and must be seen to have developed them. If they have put in genuine effort on one or more projects and have clearly communicated that they have developed their creative ability through taking part in the activity then that is the crucial – and final – 'test'.

For a few activities – playing an instrument, for example – there are national criteria such as the Grade examinations of the Royal School of Music, whilst the Duke of Edinburgh's Award Scheme offers set standards for many of the activities included in the interest section of that Scheme.

It may be, too, that a local musician or artist or a lecturer at the nearest Polytechnic would be prepared to give an expert opinion on that particular piece of work. It is hoped that we can consider assessing young people on their popular tastes in music.

Independence

This section offers Venture Scouts the opportunity to explore new areas which will help them in their future life.

They will have the chance to gain practical skills, such as budgeting, managing on a low income and finding a place to live. The section also provides opportunities to develop socially – and to gain the confidence required to make decisions about their family and their society. It is also about getting on with other people – remembering to take account of their views and to learn to be more tolerant and caring towards others.

It covers the possibilities of living with other people either as 'flat mates' or the gaining of 'skills' involved in marriage and the setting up of a home.

This section may not be able to solve all problems, but it offers the Venture Scout the opportunity to extend their own experience of life and to develop into more independent and confident people.

This section looks at the whole person – to provide him with the skills required to manage his life. The opportunities are available in this section to make him a better equipped person and to prepare him to take a more constructive role in society.

Venture Scouts may undertake activities for this section either as an individual, as a member of a group or

with the Unit as a whole. Whichever method of participation, the Unit Executive Committee must consider the contribution made by each individual Venture Scout. They also need to take into account any previous knowledge or skills in order that they may be sure that an individual has increased his knowledge and understanding in the area chosen.

To assist Unit Executive Committees in assessing this section it may be useful for them to consider the following questions about each Venture Scout's participation:

▷ Did he put into the activity sufficient effort and perseverance?

▷ What further knowledge has been gained?

▷ Did he find the activity challenging to himself?

▷ Did he improve in the activity? If so, how?

There are no right or wrong answers to the above questions as each individual is different. He may have only developed in one area – this does not matter as the individual is judged on his own progress.

International Awareness

It's a fast moving and ever changing world!

The purpose of the International Awareness section must be to help Venture Scouts to develop a greater understanding of other people and cultures and through this a greater understanding of themselves. To understand other people we need to get to know them and find out about their needs, their values, their ambitions and their beliefs. In doing so, we will also come to appreciate our own responsibilities towards other people and to our community.

An election, a famine, a riot, a new world record – all will be reported in the media across the world within seconds. All will have an impact upon our lives.

Until quite recently, especially in country areas, anyone coming from more than a few miles away was regarded as a foreigner. In our grandparents' time it was relatively rare for people to move very far away from their birthplace.

Now, however, holidays abroad and going to work in another country for a few years are both a normal part of life. We buy and use articles from all over the world – food, cars, radios, furniture – and we can eat in restaurants as diverse as Mexican and Chinese. Travel and instant communications have made the world seem smaller.

Yet there is still widespread suspicion of people from different religions, different ethnic groups or with different languages. And thousands of children die every year from hunger or preventable diseases.

Scouting is the world's largest youth organisation. More than 16 million Members in 150 countries, 1½ million Members in Europe. It thrives in all sorts of very different climates, cultures, backgrounds and social circumstances – 40% of World Scouting exists in developing countries in Africa, Asia and South America. Our organisation presents us with an unrivalled opportunity to take an active and constructive role in the development of the world community and the maintenance of peaceful and productive international relations.

To enable us to grasp this opportunity, however, we must have a knowledge and understanding of what is

going on in the world. We must appreciate the interdependence between nations and peoples and the strengths and values of other cultures.

Scouting's world-wide nature can help us to do just that.

The multi-cultural aspect of Venture Scouting is not something detached from regular life. It is not something that happens somewhere else, a long way away. It is here and now and real. It starts with you and your neighbours – and that can mean the family next door, the Unit down the road or a country in another continent.

Stage one the Unit Executive Committee, or its representative, discusses with the Venture Scouts why and how the activity will increase their multi-cultural awareness. Will it:

▷ help them to gain an understanding of other cultures and through this

▷ help them gain a greater understanding of themselves?

The activity should give the Venture Scouts a chance to improve existing skills or to gain new ones, together with (if possible) a chance to exercise leadership in a team as well as being a member of that team.

It's important to note that there is no need for the activity to be Scouting based, although many will be because of the international nature of the Movement. But that doesn't mean that a Chinese meal counts as International Awareness.

In the end, individuals should achieve the best result of which they, as individuals, are capable.

Stage two the activity itself! There are plenty of ideas in *The Venture Scout Training Scheme* but don't forget the many other opportunities for increasing International Awareness.

Stage three the assessment. In many ways this is the most difficult part of this section. But the original targets need to be discussed by the Unit Executive Committee and the Venture Scouts to see whether they all agree that they have been met. Some points which could be considered are:

▷ How have views and attitudes of the Venture Scouts changed about other cultures?

▷ What new information on other cultures have they gained and how can it be shared with others?

▷ What new skills (for example, expedition planning) have been gained?

Leadership

Venture Scouts will probably have heard of the expression 'a born leader'. Perhaps, in some cases, this statement is true, but in most instances leadership and responsibility are learned. Everyone is a potential leader given the right situation.

A responsible leader possesses a great many skills of which the following are particularly important.

The ability to:

▷ Plan

▷ Communicate

▷ Find and use resources

▷ Manage people

▷ Co-ordinate

▷ Delegate

▷ Evaluate

▷ Laugh at yourself!

The Venture Scout programme is designed to encourage and give opportunities for Venture Scouts and their friends to experience the responsibility in many forms, for example, a number of Members are required to ensure the smooth operation of the Unit by being on the Unit Executive Committee. Also, many activities will require sub-committees to see that they are conducted satisfactorily. The Unit should benefit from the leadership responsibility that comes from different Members voicing an opinion or suggesting an idea.

As part of this position of responsibility it is important to consider the wishes of the Unit and to ensure that everyone, wherever possible, can participate. Participation, commitment and communication are individual responsibilities for Unit Members and are a form of personal leadership.

The Venture Scout programme involves doing things, not just talking about them. This requires effective, responsible leadership. The experience gained in an active Unit can help Venture Scouts to take a responsible role within Scouting and society. Eventually, this experience can lead to leadership roles and personal responsibility in their future life.

Members should agree with the Unit Executive Committee the role they wish to play in the Unit and seek out appropriate training that will enable them to achieve the skills necessary. These skills should then be put into practice.

In many cases a suitable training course to provide the skills which Venture Scouts require will be readily identified. In some instances, however, the best way may be for them to devise a programme of 'in service' activity. Such a programme should be agreed with the Unit Executive Committee, Venture Scout Leader or other 'expert'.

Guidelines for assessment.
Has the Member:

▷ Undertaken training?

▷ Planned properly?

▷ Understood the tasks involved?

▷ Involved others?

▷ Used the human and material resources of the Unit?

▷ Evaluated the results of the work?

Physical, mental and spiritual development in this section needs to be drawn out in discussion with the assessing body. What has the Member gained by completing this section – how has he developed? What caused that development?

A responsible leader never becomes too solemn or takes himself too seriously. Remember Venture Scouting is supposed to be **fun**!

Outdoors and Environment

Scouting has always regarded the outdoors as a major field of activity. Baden-Powell described it as being simultaneously a laboratory, a club and a temple – a place of discovery, the setting for many Group activities and a chance for each individual to draw closer to his God. It is not surprising, therefore, that this emphasis on the outdoors should continue to feature in the Venture Scout programme.

To use the world about us is no longer sufficient, for in the last few years we have come to realise that the earth's resources are finite and, given the misuse which has occurred at the hand of man, will soon be exhausted. Combined with our enjoyment of the outdoors must, therefore, be a concern for the environment. The development

of Venture Scouts should include an appreciation of the natural world and the impact which man has on it. They should become more aware of the reasons for caring for the environment, the effects that individuals can have on it, both good and bad and the conflicts which frequently exist between human needs and the desire to prevent further misuse of it.

Venture Scouts are asked to go out and observe, try to understand or attempt to enhance some part of our environment. It will not be enough simply to go out of doors to carry out a chosen activity, Venture Scouts should also appreciate why they are doing it and the impact that it could have.

Whatever the Member chooses to do under this section it should be possible for aspects of physical, mental and spiritual development to take place.

The physical element could well concern actual physical exertion – blood, sweat and tears!

The mental development could be as simple as the detailed plan of what is to be done, how it will be achieved, the target set and the point from which the Member starts.

The factors encouraging the spiritual development are, as always, more difficult to define and to plan for – it could simply be that the area for the work is one of outstanding beauty which cries out for a silent pause in the activity to appreciate a small part of creation, it could also be the under-

standing and warmth of successful teamwork expressed over a cup of coffee late that evening.

Before the Venture Scout undertakes an activity in this section the Unit Executive Committee, or someone appointed by them, should discover from the Venture Scouts what previous experience of the activity they have had and set a target which provides a challenge and something new to achieve. In most cases this should involve about 16 hours of actual effort, perhaps over a weekend or over a longer period as required by the nature of the activity. In many cases the Unit Executive Committee will be able to gauge the achievement of the Venture Scouts by the effort that has been put into the activity, in others there will be a visible end product such as a completed project, photographic record or a verbal report to the Unit.

There should be the opportunity at the end of the activity for Venture Scouts to discuss with the Executive Committee what they have gained personally from the experience and whether it has helped their overall understanding of our environment.

Relationships

Living with other people is a continuing challenge. If the individual is ultimately to play a full part in the community then time should be spent within the Unit exchanging ideas, discovering personal needs, and finding out just what makes other people 'tick'. Units are a microcosm of the society in which the Members live and it is important for us to remember that not only are Venture Scouts learning to live with others, but they are learning to be 'liveable with'.

Different situations lead to different questions. Members on their annual expedition have the right to enjoy themselves, but do they understand the limitations imposed by locals who are not on holiday and who have their own set of rules and regulations? What are the acceptable levels of Unit Members' freedom? How do we set the Unit's and individual Member's values and behaviour norms?

Within a Unit, is there an understanding of, and an obligation to, the opposite sex? Why did she say that and he say the other? Why is it necessary to have a programme that caters for the odd-balls in the Unit? And what

makes John odder than Jill (it's worth finding out – you might just end up with John as a husband or Jill as a next door neighbour!) Are there any Members of ethnic minority within the Unit – if not, why not? There may be a very good reason. This may be a fact of life or it may be that the welcome on the mat is not obvious at all. Have we gone out of our way to absorb handicapped Members into the Unit – or should we try to?

A strong Unit does not depend on size, but rather on understanding between its Members and its acceptance within the community.

Relationships is all about the creation of these bonds between people. Assessment in this section can only be made after discussion with the Member concerned – with the Leader at a quiet moment at home or with the Unit Executive Members as they unwind over a cup of coffee and a discussion about whose turn it is to do the washing up. These can be amongst the best moments of Unit life. Interest in other people, a flexibility of understanding, a sensitivity in the handling of delicate relationships, an awareness of needs created by the environment and an ability to stand in the other fellow's shoes are all of greater value than social achievements. The completion of a project without 'why?' being asked or answered is a negation of this section. Personal growth of the Member must be paramount.

The emphasis in this section needs to be concerned with:

▷ Sharing with others

▷ Caring for others

▷ Tolerance of others and their different viewpoints

▷ Understanding the other's point of view

▷ Helping others to understand your views

▷ Team building

▷ Courtesy and thought

Values

How often will a Venture Scout have heard someone else expressing a strongly held view and thought 'there must be more to this' or do they have a strongly held view because they know it's right but feel that they would like to know more about the issue so that they can express themselves better. This section of the Venture Scout Award gives them the opportunity to develop their own views on an issue after finding out the facts and considering other people's opinions.

Their views and feelings on an issue are their own and no-one should tell them how to think or what to believe in. But sometimes they will have to reconsider a particular point of view in the light of experiences or because society changes but when they do, it is important that they have the ability to recognise why their views are changing and be able to justify a shift in opinion, if only to themselves!

After choosing an area in which they are particularly interested the Member should ensure that they consider a wide range of opinions on the subject. They should look at it from as many different angles as they can, either by talking to others or reading and so on. When they feel that they have the facts, they must consider them all, think about why someone holds a particular view, not just dismissing it because it does not agree with other views, or because the opinion was not expressed very well. They should try to keep an open mind (no easy task when quite often many issues cause people to hold extreme views, which they can express very forcibly!).

The next stage is to consider how they feel about the subject or issue. Most issues do not have a right or wrong answer, only a range of opinions. It must be down to them to consider what they feel is 'right'. This, perhaps, is the most difficult part. It is easy for Venture Scouts to be influenced by others but very difficult for them to stand back and consider how they feel in themselves.

The final stage is for Venture Scouts to share their findings with another person or group of people. The discussion should cover:

▷ Why they chose that subject

▷ How they gathered the facts and opinions

▷ What they have learned about the subject and themselves

▷ What conclusions they have come to.

There may, of course, be things that they found out about themselves that they do not want to share. That's OK, but encourage them to try, it is often useful and interesting to talk to others.

Finally, Venture Scouts should not try to let this be a 'one-off' exercise, they could consider other issues as they arise in their lives. Remember that they, and the society in which they live, are continually changing

When assessing a Venture Scout for this section of the Award, the Unit Executive should always bear in mind they are considering someone else's personal views and values. We are all different people with different experiences and consequently different views. There is quite often no right or wrong answer, just differing opinions – and we must respect these differences even if sometimes the views expressed contradict our own.

Any activity in this section should be followed by an opportunity to express what has been learned about the issue or subject, what the person has learned about themselves and what views have been formed about the issue.

Some helpful questions to consider may be:

▷ Why was this subject or issue chosen?

▷ Has the whole range of opinions on the issue been considered?

▷ What has the Venture Scout learned about himself?

▷ Have their views altered? If so, why?

▷ What conclusions have been arrived at?

▷ How do they feel this will help them in the future?

and developing and their views and values should be reconsidered in the light of developments – not changed necessarily – just thought about from time to time. Hopefully by completing this section of the Award they will have the ability to consider a whole range of issues and so develop their own opinions and standards whilst being tolerant of others who may hold alternative points of view.

The Queen's Scout Award

This, the première Award for Members of the Association in the Training Scheme, like the Venture Scout Award, needs some planning from the Venture Scouts themselves along with the support of the Venture Scout Leader and the Unit Executive Committee.

It must be remembered that whilst the first requirement states that Venture Scouts must hold the Venture Scout Award, it is *not* a pre-requisite – Venture Scouts do not have to gain the Venture Scout Award before attempting the requirements of the Queen's Scout Award – they can be done alongside each other, some before or some afterwards.

The emphasis is placed so that the Unit Executive Committee play a very full part in the operation and assessment of the Queen's Scout Award. They monitor progress and offer assistance, they approve (or otherwise) schemes to gain the individual facets of the Award and in the end they, after an interview between the District Commissioner and the Venture Scout concerned, take the decision to make the Award or not. It is hoped that the Venture Scout Leader will play a part in the procedure offering experience and advice.

Within the Award there is great scope for leadership and service, both to the community and within Scouting and opportunities should be taken to encourage Venture Scouts to play a full part in this aspect.

It is expected that Venture Scouts will be able to achieve this Award (along with the Venture Scout Award) after some three to four years of Unit Membership.

Rule 124
The Queen's Scout Award

To be passed under arrangements made by the Unit Executive Committee and awarded by them after consultation with the Venture Scout Leader and the District Commissioner (following his informal interview with the Venture Scout).

A gold crown with ornamentation on a brown background with a white border.

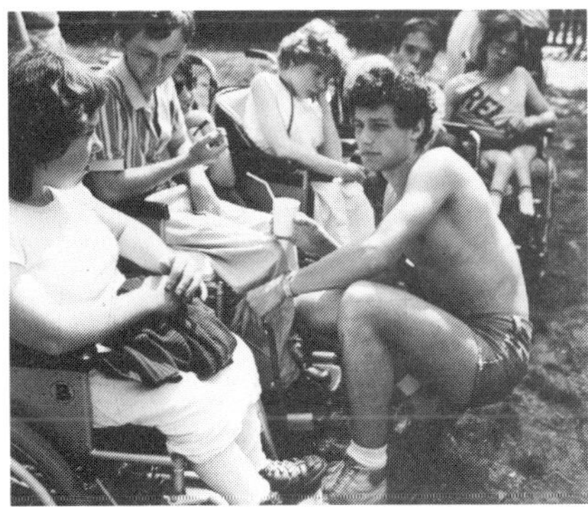

Requirements

Rule 124 i

1 **Hold the Venture Scout Award**

2 **Community – Training and Involvement**
   (complete a & b)

2a Training
Undertake training in helping the community in such fields as:

▶ rescue (for example, cave, mountain, beach, fire, coastguard or canoe) or emergency aid services:

▶ first aid to the standard of an appropriate qualification of the St John Ambulance Association, British Red Cross Society or St Andrew's Ambulance Association or if gained for the Venture Scout Award, an additional qualification of the same voluntary aid agency:

▶ lifesaving (for example, qualifying for the bronze medallion of the Royal Lifesaving Society or, if gained for the Venture Scout Award, for the Award of Merit of the Royal Lifesaving Society):

▶ specialist training (for example, to help the blind, elderly, mentally or physically handicapped):

▶ specialist activity as an instructor, (for example, canoe instructor, Sunday School teacher or Football Association referee):

▶ other forms of community service training as approved by the Unit Executive Committee.

2b Involvement
Over a sustained period (for example 36 hours) undertake practical effort to help the community. Depending upon local needs, this may be spread over several months or take a more concentrated form. The service might be one of the following:

▶ in the local community – such as working in a hospital, assisting in the work of your place of worship, helping with handicapped children, helping to run an adventure playground or a cycling proficiency scheme:

► working on conservation projects – such as with the Conservation Corps or National Trust, helping to restore inland waterways, narrow gauge railways or some form of industrial archaeology, improving National Parks, camp sites or derelict city areas:

► helping staff to maintain a permanent camp site or activity centre, running a Group or District magazine for six months, providing specialist skills as an instructor, for example in swimming, canoeing or photography, up to Scout proficiency badge standards:

► helping with some form of social service or work camp at home or abroad, arranged by a local authority or voluntary organisation:

► other forms of community service as approved by the Unit Executive Committee.

3 Leadership
(complete a or b)

Undertake a leadership or similarly responsible role in an aspect of your community or Scouting. Undertake appropriate training as necessary. This should be arranged in consultation with the Unit Executive Committee and the Venture Scout Leader.

3a Within Scouting
for example

► lead a team of Unit Members and, in consultation with the Assistant District Commissioner (Scouts), appropriate Scout Leaders and Patrol Leaders' Councils, organise and run a number of Meetings for Scout Troops in the District: or

► provide at least six months' practical service as an Instructor or Assistant Leader in a Scout Troop, Cub Scout Pack or Beaver Scout Colony: or

► devise, organise and lead a residential Venture Scout introductory course over two nights for older Scouts: or

► undertake responsibility in the organisation and implementation of some form of Executive Committee training or Leadership Training within your Unit District or County/Area: or

► fulfill the responsibilities of a key post as an elected Member of the Unit Executive Committee. This role should involve a greater commitment than

any previous responsibility already undertaken in the Venture Scout Award.

3b In the Community
for example

▶ serve as a member of your local community council or local youth council playing a full part over a period of at least one year undertaking appropriate training as suggested by a youth officer or equivalent: or

▶ serve as an office bearer in a local or national voluntary organisation such as the Auxiliary Fire Service, Emergency Aid Team or Council of Social Services undertaking an appropriate course of training: or

▶ undertake a leadership role within the 'junior club' of a local youth centre or youth club on a voluntary basis and complete suitable youth service training arranged by the local authority.

4 Pursuit or Interest
(complete a or b)

4a Pursuit
Reach a reasonable standard in a physical or creative pursuit, sport or hobby. This can be either an entirely new activity or an existing one developed to a higher level of achievement.

Note:
Suggestions on standards appropriate are available in The Duke of Edinburgh's Award Handbook.

4b Interest
Undertake two further items from different areas of the Venture Scout Award. These items must be different from those used to qualify for the Venture Scout Award.

5 Exploration – Training and Expedition
(complete a, b & c)

5a Training

Carry out suitable training appropriate to the type of expedition you intend to undertake. This must include practice expeditions, lightweight camping experience, selection of correct clothing and equipment, load carrying, food, cooking, hygiene, map reading and compass work, route planning, leading a party, accident precautions and procedures, expedition first aid. This training must be approved by the Unit Executive Committee.

5b Expedition

Plan and undertake an expedition with a purpose over at least three nights and four days in unfamiliar and challenging country. This must be approved by the Unit Executive Committee.

for example:

▶ on foot – 80 kilometres (50 miles) in wild country with a small group (between four and seven in number):

▶ by cycle – 335 kilometres (210 miles) including rural areas:

▶ by canoe, raft or punt – (no set distance, but at least six hours paddling, rafting or punting time per day) on suitable inland waterways or sheltered coastal waters:

▶ on horseback – 160 kilometres (100 miles) including bridle paths and trackless sections of wild country.

5c Report

Make a formal presentation or report of your expedition to the Unit. This could take the form of a log book, tape/slide presentation, video film and so on but must reflect the purpose of the expedition.

Notes:

(i) Enterprising expeditions abroad are encouraged. Distances can be varied according to local conditions of climate and terrain, but they must involve the party in careful preparation, physical effort and sustained endeavour in an area unknown to Members.

(ii) Mixed expeditions are acceptable.

(iii) In individual cases where a four day expedition is not feasible then two linked expeditions of shorter duration are permissible at the discretion of the Unit Executive Committee.

(iv) The Activity Rules of The Scout Association **must** *be followed when planning and implementing any option in this section.*

(v) Venture Scouts wishing to complete this section alongside the Duke of Edinburgh's Award (Gold) should consult the Handbook of that Scheme before starting.

6 Assessment and Interview

On completion of the above requirements, the Venture Scout must arrange for an informal interview with the District Commissioner to discuss these achievements and future plans. The District Commissioner will pass his comments to the Unit Executive Committee who will also consult with the Venture Scout Leader in reaching their final decision on making the Award.

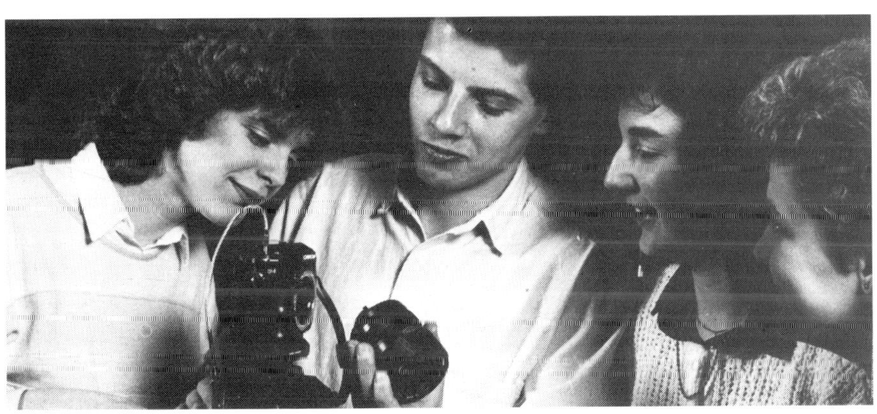

Guidance for the Queen's Scout Award

1 Hold the Venture Scout Award
Enough is already said within previous pages with reference to this initial requirement.

2 Community
2a Training
The criteria for this sub-section are that the training must be worthwhile, recognisable and usable. There is little point in a Member gaining the training qualification if he is not going to be able to use it. Thus, when selecting the form of training the Venture Scout concerned should endeavour to find a course or in-service scheme that suits their interests and skills.

2b Involvement
This sub-section demands a high level of community involvement. Although the example of 36 hours seems short it is up to the Unit Executive Committee to ensure that the service is worthwhile, fulfilling and of use to the community. The service could be in concentrated form over a short intensive period, for example, a special

work camp or a long weekend – or
spread out over six months at the rate
of one and a half hours every Wednes-
day evening. The type of service
provided will usually dictate the timescale. Whilst this basic format covers
the Award itself it is hoped that
Members undertaking this service
will not just stop when the required
number of hours have been completed
– the continuation of the work will not
only aid the agency concerned but will
add to the Members' understanding
and involvement.

3 Leadership

This sub-section requires a Member
to find a responsible leadership role
within the community or Scouting and
to choose some form of appropriate
training. The training could be pre-
training, in-service or on-going
depending upon the desires of the
Member and the needs of the job. The
main criterion is that a leadership role
should have been successfully carried
out for about 36 hours, either in a
concentrated form, for example, a
long weekend or over a longer period

spread out over a number of weeks as required – with the Member having undergone training to suit the role.

In determining what is appropriate, the time devoted must be sufficient to allow the Venture Scout to:

▷ Fulfil the chosen role

▷ Show a commitment to the others involved

▷ Play a significant part in the activity

▷ Show improved performance over the period selected.

A note of caution should be added when referring to undertaking Leader Training for Leadership within Scouting.

Venture Scout Leaders and Unit Executive Committees should ensure that the Members concerned have the desire and commitment to assist with Colonies, Packs or Troops and are not just doing it to get the badge.

4 Pursuits or interests

Where Members wish to try a new activity a reasonable standard should apply (for example, the British Canoe Union 2 or 3 Star Award – depending upon competence), but where an existing activity is utilised, and may have been for the Venture Scout Award, at least the next stage higher should be completed (for example, a rock climber who can already climb successfully to severe grades on single pitch faces should be able to complete a climb to perhaps very severe, or hard very severe on single pitch).

The Venture Scout who has appeared on stage in a small part and chorus items should, for this section, be able to undertake a leading role in a production or use their skills by being a stage manager or lighting controller and so on. If Venture Scouts decide to undertake two items from

the Venture Scout Award then they are expected to enter fully into the activity chosen. Assessment would then be as for that section of the Venture Scout Award.

5 Exploration

It cannot be emphasised too much that the training must cover all the eventualities and should be led by a competent person. It is the duty of the Unit Executive Committee to ensure that the training is suitable and thorough and that the choice of expedition is practical and realistic for the Members concerned.

It is not suitable, for example, for Venture Scouts to go to a hazardous area when they are not experienced, trained or physically fit enough to do so. Unit Executives should be quite prepared to refuse permission for the expedition and to suggest alternative routes, areas and so on. Unit Executive Committees should ensure that note (*iv*) is adhered to in all cases – especially see *Policy, Organisation and Rules* under the following:

▷ Expeditions

▷ Activities on the land

▷ Activities on the water

▷ Riding

6 Assessment and Interview
The Unit Executive Committee will
need to check that the District
Commissioner is satisfied that the
Venture Scout has made personal
progress. They should then, in conjunction with the Venture Scout
Leader, discuss the Member's Award
in the light of his abilities, efforts and
attainments. Guidance for the assessment of awards is given in the publication *The Venture Scout Training
Scheme*.

Presentation of the Queen's Scout Award

The Queen's Scout Award badge
should be presented by the County or
Area Commissioner or his delegate at
a special Group or District occasion.
Whenever possible, Queen's Scouts
should also attend a special reception
to receive their Royal Certificates from
the Chief Scout. When this is not
possible, the Royal Certificates should
be presented at a suitable occasion by
a person of appropriate standing such
as the Chief Commissioner or the
Lord Lieutenant of a County.

It is hoped that the Queen's Scouts
will attend the annual National Scout
Service at Windsor. This Service and
Parade is held every April in the
Quadrangle and St George's Chapel
within Windsor Castle.

Bibliography

The following publications are available to assist with all aspects of Venture Scouting:

The Venture Scout Series – published by The Scout Association

The Venture Scout Training Scheme

Publicity, Public Relations and Recruitment by J. N. Barr

Constitutions, Committees and Chairmen by J. N. Barr

The Role of the Leader by John Beresford

Creativity by Michael Beach

Programme Planning by Alan Vince

Community Involvement by David Bull

Expeditions by Peter G. Drake

Our Multi-cultural Society by Gilly Greensitt

Starting a Venture Scout Unit by J. N. Barr

What's all this about God? by Father Roger Barralet, OFM

Other useful publications

The Youth Games Book by Alan Dearling and Howard Armstrong, published by the IT Resource Centre

The Youth Arts and Craft Book by Alan Dearling and Howard Armstrong, published by the IT Resource Centre

Leaving Home by Alan Dearling and Mark Clark, published by the IT Resource Centre

First Aid Manual – published by St John Ambulance, St Andrew's Ambulance and the British Red Cross Society

Expedition Guide – published by The Duke of Edinburgh's Award Scheme

Canoeing Handbook – published by the British Canoe Union

Energise – published by The Scout Association

Mountaincraft and Leadership by Eric Langmuir, published by the Mountain Leader Training Board

The Backpacker's Handbook by Derrick Booth, published by Charles Letts and Co. Ltd.

First Aid for Hillwalkers by Jane Renouf and Steward Huise, published by Cicerone Press

Modern Rope Techniques by Bill March, published by Cicerone Press

It's not fair! – a handbook on world development for youth groups – published by Christian Aid

16 Up – published by the National
Youth Bureau

*Under 18 – a guide to the law as it
affects young people* – published by the
Citizens Advice Bureau and the
National Youth Bureau

*Drug misuse and the young – a guide
for teachers and youth workers* –
published by the Department of
Education and Science
(available free)

Counselling young people by Tom
Wylie, published by the National Youth
Bureau

Prayers for life by Michel Quoist,
published by Gill and Macmillan

Safety on Mountains – published by
the British Mountaineering Council

Notes for Guiders on religious faith –
published by The Girl Guides
Association

What to do about glue-sniffing –
published by the Health Education
Council
(available free)

Mountain Navigation by Peter Cliff,
published by Cordee Books